Minute Motivators for Athletes

*Quick Inspiration for the
Time of Your Life*

Stan Toler
Billy Bajema

To Travis,

Bill B 47

06 05 04 03 02   10 9 8 7 6 5 4 3 2 1

Minute Motivators for Athletes
ISBN: 978-1-937602-26-0
Copyright © 2012 by Stan Toler & Billy Bajema

Dust Jacket Press
PO Box 721243
Oklahoma City, OK 73172
www.dustjacket.com <http://www.dustjacket.com>
800-495-0192

Contents

Introduction

It should come as no surprise that the Bible is full of references to athletes. Sports serve as a powerful metaphor for our spiritual life. Just as athletes must be driven and focused and determined, so followers of Jesus must devote their lives to Him in order to achieve the prize.

Athletes need special encouragement for their day-to-day lives because they cannot afford to take a break from the lifestyle required for excellence in their sport. Even when it's not race day, athletes are training and eating right and gearing up psychologically for the big event. That requires perseverance, which cannot be mustered up by sheer will power alone. You need something more. You need inspiration.

Minute Motivators for Athletes is a source of encouragement and inspiration for men and women of any age who have chosen to use their bodies to the full potential that God has given.

See you at the finish line!

—Stan Toler & Billy Bajema

Be relaxed.

Do not let what you cannot do interfere

with what you can do.

—John Wooden

SELF-ACCEPTANCE

Every athlete is meticulously scrutinized by coaches, judges, fans, friends, and even relatives. It's the nature of the role. You train to perform, and performance is for an audience. Being constantly judged has to affect your psyche—unless you intentionally resist its power. If you were to allow other people's opinion of you to shape your opinion of self, the stress would be too much. You would constantly be riding highs and lows, and working in vain for acceptance.

Resist the temptation to judge your self-worth based on the opinions of other people. While it is important to honor the legitimate expectations of your coach and teammates, constantly seeking approval leads to a life of frustration. The highs will be high—when others affirm you. But the lows will be even lower when they do not. Your spiritual and emotional well-being will be diminished, and your athletic performance will suffer.

Just relax. Take a deep breath, and enjoy what you're doing. Pay attention to the thing that made you fall in love with sports in the first place. Take pleasure in the fact that you have a strong, fit, and healthy body. Feel the satisfaction as you push yourself to excel. Enjoy the thrill of the game. Celebrate your successes. And thank God for your skill.

Keep getting better.

Nobody's a natural. You work hard to get good and then work to get better. It's hard to stay on top.

—Paul Coffey

ACHIEVEMENT

Achieving things that at one time seemed impossible is one of the most fulfilling aspects of being an athlete. You may have achieved a childhood dream of making your high school team. Now it's time to set your sights even higher. Maybe you want to be a starter, earn a college scholarship, or help lead your team to a state championship. God created us to live with a purpose. If you're not working to get better in whatever you do you're wasting your time. And time is precious! There are many great things to strive for and it feels good when goals are reached, but real joy is in the struggle. Holding up the trophy is nice, but the greatest memories have more to do with the steps taken to get there.

The adage is true that if you're not getting better, you're getting worse.Complacency kills progress and even kick starts the reverse process into action.If you get to the point where you think you've arrived, you're probably beginning your descent.Great athletes know that there is always room for improvement.

Don't settle! Continue to work on all aspects of your performance—physical conditioning, technique, knowledge, and endurance. Your achievement in sports will be a direct result of your willingness to develop yourself. Work hard, and you will succeed!

Be a great teammate.

Nobody's more important

than the team.

—RejeanHoule

UNITY

Most athletes hold to the ideal of the rugged individualist. We envision ourselves as the one crossing the finish line, hitting in the winning run, or standing alone on the podium. There is something about sport that brings out the individual in us. We value the solo contribution. That bent toward an independent spirit is a constant temptation for athletes. When we achieve, we tend to think we can go it alone. We may start believing that we are being held back by the mistakes of others. It is easy to place ourselves ahead of the team.

Yet the idea of the lone champion is a myth. In addition to the nine players on a baseball field, there are thirty-one others in reserve. Even a marathoner depends on coaches, trainers, equipment manufacturers, and other support personnel. No athlete can go it alone! Worse, when we see ourselves as better or more needed than the team, we poison the atmosphere in which we must train and compete. We need unity in order to succeed.

Resist the temptation to go it alone. A team with great athletes who don't work together will lose to a team of mediocre talents whose hearts beat as one. Never lose sight of the value of your teammates, coaches, trainers, and friends. You will need all of them if you are to win. Success in sport cannot be achieved by athleticism alone. It takes a team.

Listen to your coach.

Coaches have to watch for what they
don't want to see and listen to what
they don't want to hear.

—John Madden

TRUST

It happens to every athlete at some point. It may come after your first few seasons, when you have begun to achieve success. Or it could happen when there is a change in leadership and your seasoned coach is replaced by a rookie. Every athlete eventually faces the moment when he or she distrusts the direction of the coach. We believe that we know more, understand the game better, read our opponents more clearly, or are more in tune with our teammates. When that happens, you will face one of the critical moments in the development of every athlete. You must learn to trust.

The price of doubt or rebellion will be high. A team can have only one final authority, and even solo athletes have difficulty assessing things objectively. We need the wisdom, expertise, and guidance of another. Disregard the coach's training regimen, and your performance will suffer. Defy the coach's instructions, and your team will splinter. Rebellion is not a pathway to success.

When you find yourself in conflict with your coach, always give your leader the respect he or she deserves. Realize that coaches see things from a more objective vantage point, have a better knowledge of the game, and really do have your best interests at heart. Love them or hate them, you must always respect them. You really do need your coach.

Dream big.

Sooner or later, those who win are
those who think they can.

—Richard Bach

IMAGINATION

Many athletes fail not because they lack talent but because they lack imagination. God wants us to have great vision, not for personal glory but to achieve, grow, and contribute to the world. You are an athlete, and God gifted you with the skill you have. He wants you to use it to your fullest potential so that you will bring glory to Him and delight to others. What is possible for you? Where will your talents and determination take you?

Remember that the purpose of your achievement is not for you alone. God did not create us to bring glory to ourselves but to bring glory and honor to Him. It is a mistake to dream dreams for ourselves alone. If your vision for the future includes only you, your dream is selfish. Imagine how your achievements can be used to honor God, uplift others, or enrich your community.

Don't be afraid to dream! Think of all that you could accomplish with God's blessing on your hard work and skill. Really. Go ahead and dream. What could you achieve if you dedicated yourself fully to your sport? What milestones have never been achieved in your sport? Could you reach them? Having vision leads you to great places. So let your imagination lead you.

Love discipline.

A pint of sweat will save

a gallon of blood.

—George Patton

SELF-DISCIPLINE

Most athletes live for game day; few are motivated to hit the practice field. Training is routine, repetitive, and sometimes painful. Swim workouts at 5:00 a.m., three-a-day's on the football field, stretching, drills, warm-ups, cool-downs: these things aren't always enjoyable but they're always worth it. We do them not because they are pleasant but because they produce the result we are after—victory!

And there is a hidden benefit to the disciplines of sport. That discipline will transfer to other areas of life. Being able to control yourself—to do the hard thing, to deny yourself, to press on—is also a value in relationships, friendship, marriage, and employment. The payoff is a deeper relationship with others and a higher degree of trust. People respect someone who is self-disciplined. There is a personal value as well. If you are disciplined in training, you will likely be disciplined in eating, spending, and academics. Self-discipline is the foundation for a successful life.

So go ahead and set that alarm for 5:00 a.m. Hit the gym even when you'd rather hit the couch. Get on the bike and do the miles. Push yourself! If you can discipline yourself physically you will be a winner—in competition and in life.

Be loyal.

Friendships born on the field of athletic strife are the real golf of competition. Awards become corroded, friends gather no dust.

—Jesse Owens

FRIENDSHIP

One of the joys of athletics is the camaraderie that develops among fellow athletes, teammates, and coaches. There is something about the intensity of physical competition that forges deep and lasting relationships. When you suffer through workouts together, endure the long bus rides, and experience the highs and lows of a competitive season, you develop a trust and loyalty with your teammates that can last a lifetime.

Respect those relationships, and don't allow your competitive spirit to dampen them. The desire to achieve has led some athletes to sacrifice family relationships, friendships, and even their own integrity in pursuit of winning. No athletic goal is worth the price of loyalty. Friends are more valuable than trophies. Keep relationships and winning in the right order—relationships first.

This takes effort. Few of us are naturally inclined to place the interests of others ahead of our own. It takes strength of character to put other people first. The good news is that this strength is accessible to everyone; it just takes a decision to implement it, and a little motivation to sustain it. When you hang up the cleats, there is something you will remember even more fondly than your greatest victory: the friends who were there to celebrate it with you. Remember the priority—relationships first.

Keep sports in perspective.

Be more concerned with your character than your reputation, because your character is what you really are, while your reputation is merely what others think you are.

—John Wooden

PRIORITIES

Perhaps you have known an athlete like the man I'll call Jason. Jason was in his mid-thirties, a software engineer with a Fortune 500 company, and about forty pounds overweight. Fortunately Jason decided to tackle his weight problem and took up running. As the pounds came off, Jason became more and more involved in the sport. He entered a 5K, then a 10K, and finally decided to train for a half-marathon. Within just a few years, Jason was in the form of his life and was competing in one or two triathlons a year. There was only one problem—Jason's personal life was disintegrating. His career had stalled, and his wife had filed for divorce. Jason had allowed his sport to become his obsession.

Sport is a means to enhance our lives. It disciplines us physically, challenges us mentally, and sharpens our competitive edge—all good things. Yet sport is not an end in itself. No sport can bring meaning to our lives, be our companion, or comfort us in our old age. Sport is a great avocation or even a good profession. It will never be a friend.

Here's a short list of the things that matter in life: God, integrity, family, character, community, friendships, and peace. Let your sport support your main priorities—not replace them.

Eat right.

Do not join those who drink too much wine or gorge themselves on meat, for drunkards and gluttons become poor, and drowsiness clothes them in rags.

— Proverbs 23:20-21

NUTRITION

Garbage in, garbage out. That adage tells us how computers work. What you get out of them depends on the quality of the data that you put in. You cannot expect to get accurate answers from flawed data or bug-ridden programs. To gain top results you must feed the machine with high-quality information. Your body works in exactly the same way. Your performance is directly tied to your diet. If you nourish yourself with high-fat, high-carb, low-protein junk food, your athletic performance will suffer immediately. Garbage in, garbage out. Correspondingly, when you eat properly, your body will respond positively. Your performance will increase.

For most of us, though, the act of eating is more than just taking on nutrition. We eat to celebrate, to comfort ourselves, to relax, and to just plain enjoy the experience! That makes diet a difficult area for the athlete to control. What happens on the field, we can manage pretty well. But eating takes place in personal and social settings. You need to be disciplined there too.

Don't allow your stomach to undo all the hard work you've put into training! Consult a nutritionist or study the literature on nutrition for your sport. Learn to control your appetite for unwholesome foods—and especially alcohol. Eat healthy, and you will gain energy for sport and for life.

Be humble.

Pride goes before destruction, a
haughty spirit before a fall.

—Proverbs 16:18

PERSPECTIVE

"**I** am the greatest!" When Muhammad Ali said those words as a twenty-two-year-old world champion, he stood at the beginning of a promising career as a prizefighter. Yet the same Ali who was so prone to outrageous statements that he was dubbed "the Louisville Lip" later said this: "A man who views the world the same at fifty as he did at twenty has wasted thirty years of his life." Clearly, the champ had learned to place life and sport in proper perspective.

Most athletes would love to be able to make Ali's boast: "I am the greatest." We all have a desire to win. We want to distinguish ourselves, to achieve, to be on top in our sport. Some of us will be fortunate enough to receive those accolades. You may have the opportunity to stand atop the podium, hoist a trophy, or be interviewed on the six o'clock news. With success comes honor, and that honor may be yours.

When that time comes, remember that you will be then the same person that you are today. Your success will not be yours alone; it will be shared with all who helped you achieve. And you are not the sum of your awards and honors. Give credit to others. Share your achievement. Be humble. That is the greatest honor of all.

Maximize your potential.

I want to be remembered as the
guy who gave his all whenever
he was on the field.

—Walter Payton

EFFICIENCY

Not every activity that is worth doing is worth *your* time and energy. Some training regimens have little payoff. What works for other athletes may not work for you. You simply can't do everything. The problem is that there are lots of good things that clamor for your attention and other fun or interesting things that you would like to do.

Here's what happens if you do not learn to be efficient with your time and energy. You avoid some of the soreness the next day, but you don't gain that last 5 percent of performance. You explore lots of possibilities for being active in your sport, but you don't focus on the single skill or event where you have the greatest potential. You are part of the team and have a good time with your friends, but never know what it feels like to stand on the field victorious after giving everything you have toward your goal. That's the cost of wasting even one ounce of your God-given potential. Your time, energy, and opportunities are like gold. You need every ounce of them in order to succeed.

God made you as a unique individual, loaded with potential. Make the most of your days. Maximize every opportunity. Train smart. Never pass up an opportunity to do something vital to pursue something that is merely interesting. Your time is too valuable to waste.

Concentrate.

Mental will is a muscle that
needs exercise, just like
muscles of the body.

—Lynn Jennings

FOCUS

Your life is filled with distractions. If your home is average, the television is on for at least four hours each day. By some estimates, you are exposed to more than three thousand advertising messages every twenty-four hours. In addition to these diversions, you have real responsibilities that claim your attention as a parent, a spouse, an employee, a student. If you are going to succeed at your sport, you must learn to focus.

Lack of focus is often the difference between finishing well and not finishing at all. Teams that lack focus begin to squabble amongst themselves. Athletes who lack focus back off on their training, cheat on their diet, or let up—just for a moment— during competition. The ability to concentrate does not ensure that you will win, but a failure to concentrate almost guarantees that you will lose.

Concentration is a skill that must be learned like any other. Everyone has to learn the discipline of shutting out distractions. When you are training, set your mind on the most important goal for that day, then refuse to allow your attention to wander until it is accomplished. When you are competing, ruthlessly drive from your mind any thought that takes you away from your goal. Narrow your vision, focus your thoughts, and stick with the task.

Have a great attitude.

Sooner or later, those who win are
those who think they can.

—Richard Bach

OPTIMISM

Attitude is a little thing that makes a big difference. When you study the people who have succeeded in any area of life, you will find that they all have one thing in common—a positive attitude! Critics don't create great achievements, they find fault with them. Complainers don't accomplish big things, they look for reasons why success is impossible. To succeed in sport—or in anything—you must have a positive outlook.

Maintaining that outlook won't always be easy. In fact, you will be challenged in this area almost every day of your life. There will be challenges. You will find obstacles in your path. You will suffer injury, disappointment, pain, and frustration. When that happens you will face a choice that will define your life as an athlete and as a person. You can choose to see the future as bleak, doubtful, and filled with problems. Or you can choose to see the possibilities hiding behind the problems.

Choose to have a positive outlook. It *is* a choice you can make. Believe that the future is always brighter than the past. Accept the idea that your best opportunities are still in front of you. Make the decision to focus on what's right with yourself, with others, and with your situation. Keep your spirits high, and your prospects will follow!

Do it!

You miss 100 percent of the

shots you never take.

—Wayne Gretzky

WORK ETHIC

The hardest part of any endeavor is getting started. For an athlete, that means that the hardest part of any workout is getting yourself to the gym, or getting on the bike, or getting into the pool. If you consistently have the self-discipline to get out there and train, you will consistently improve, consistently compete, and consistently win. Though it has become cliché to say it, when it comes to sport the best advice is "Just do it!"

Every day you will find a hundred reasons for not pushing yourself to give that extra effort. It's a bye week, so there's no urgency to train. You did the extra reps yesterday, so you can skip today. You're already working harder than anyone else on the team, why dig for the extra seconds? These are the voices that will pull you away from being your best, both in training and in competition. Never allow that thinking to disrupt your concentration or degrade your work ethic. You're better than that.

Go hard at it every day. Sure, there are days when you're due for a lighter workout or a rest day. But never back off from offering your best. Give 100 percent effort in every lap, every rep, every mile. Work hard, not for your coach or trainer or even your competitors. Do it for yourself.

Hold your head up.

Nobody who ever gave his
best regretted it.

—George Halas

SELF-RESPECT

It is going to happen sometime. Not every time, but sometime. You're going to lose. Very few competitors in any sport have been undefeated throughout their career, or even for a single season. Losing is a fact of life in sport. On any given day, another team may be stronger, another athlete may be faster or better or just plain luckier. Every competitor must find a way to deal with losing without losing his or her self-respect.

The secret is to give your best effort every time you take the field. Always be prepared, always be trained, always have a game plan, always execute to the best of your ability. You cannot control the conditions, the competition, or the calls. But you can ensure that you have given your best performance in every contest. When that is true, you will never have a reason to hang your head. There is no shame in not being the best competitor on a given day. The only shame is in not giving your best effort.

So train well. Work hard. Compete with intensity. Give all of your heart and mind to the battle. And when you walk off the court, or climb out of the pool, or exit the track, hold your head high. You are worthy of respect.

Find a coach.

Plans fail for lack of counsel, but
with many advisers they succeed.

—Proverbs 15:22

TEACHABILITY

It is like a disease in sport. The brightest talents seem to suffer from it the most. Those blessed with natural ability are nearly always afflicted with this problem. It is the idea that talent is enough, that you are doing well enough on your own, that you can do it by yourself. The truth is that every athlete needs a coach. We simply cannot see ourselves objectively. We cannot fully assess our own strengths and weaknesses, or see how to improve. No one can. That's why we need a coach.

Teachability is not an asset in your athletic career alone. It is a spiritual virtue that will aid you in becoming a more complete child of God, a better spouse, and a more valuable employee. The refusal to listen or take advice from others is a significant handicap in any area of life. It is a form of pride that can be very destructive. To be teachable, humble, and open to change is a great virtue.

Who is coaching your athletic performance? If you are an amateur athlete, you can still find good coaching. If you cannot hire a coach, find a more seasoned athlete who can work with you, or find a partner with whom you can share knowledge and advice. You need a guide who can help you along the way.

Improve your strengths.

A winner is someone who recognizes
his God-given talents, works his tail off
to develop them into skills, and uses
these skills to accomplish his goals.

—Larry Bird

PROGRESS

What are you best at? What are your top three strengths as an athlete? Maybe it's speed, or ability, or strength, or endurance. One key to success in sport is to find out what your strengths are and improve them. If you're not sure what your best gifts are, ask a coach or even a competitor. Others can probably see your performance more objectively than you can. Once you find your greatest concentration of strengths, work to improve them.

That sounds simple, but it is not what most athletes do. We tend to major on our weaknesses, spending more time trying to improve the areas in which our capacity is limited. If we lack speed, we do speed drills. If our hitting is suspect, we spend extra time in the batting cage. That's counterproductive. Your best option is to *minimize* your weaknesses and *maximize* your strengths.

Do you know what your best skills are? Now it's time to improve them. If your long suit is endurance, train even harder in that area. If you win by having great field awareness, study the game even more thoroughly. If you can shoot well, take extra shooting drills. Your greatest potential for gain lies in improving the things at which you already excel.

Minimize your weaknesses.

Do not let what you cannot do interfere with what you can do.

—John Wooden

ADVANTAGE

Every athlete has weaknesses; there are no supermen or super women. Reggie Jackson was a great slugger, but he struck out 2,597 times, more than any other major league player in history. Michael Jordan may be the greatest basketball player ever to step on the court. Yet his short-lived baseball career was a disaster. No athlete can do it all. We all have areas of weakness that hinder our performance.

The key to success is not to focus on those weaknesses but to minimize them. If your vertical leap is only eighteen inches, forget about going up for the rebound. Concentrate on court position instead. If you love to cycle but are two hundred pounds of solid muscle, you'll probably never make a great climber. Rather than waste time trying to improve that area, choose flat races and work on your sprinting. It is tempting to believe that you can turn every weakness into a strength, but it is not likely to happen.

Don't allow your weaknesses to take away your competitive advantage. Give up on the idea that you can be the perfect athlete. Accept that there are some things you simply don't do well. Give your weaknesses just enough attention so that they don't handicap you completely. Then work on ways to minimize their impact. Surround your weaknesses with your strengths.

Play for something greater.

If all I'm remembered for is being a
good basketball player, then I've done
a bad job with the rest of my life.

—Isiah Thomas

CONTRIBUTION

The world of sport is filled with stories of great athletes who were not great human beings. Some were great talents who believed that their athletic gifts excused their lack of integrity. Others were so singly devoted to their sport that they ignored relationships. Their victories came at the expense of their families. Athletic success requires great focus and dedication. Unfortunately, that dedication can come at the expense of other meaningful things in life.

Many great athletes, however, have set an example of character in sports and in life. Peyton Manning's PeyBack Foundation promotes the future success of disadvantaged youth by assisting programs that provide leadership and growth opportunities for children at risk. Lance Armstrong's Livestrong Foundation helps to improve the lives of people affected by cancer. You don't have to make a choice between being a great athlete and a great human being.

Live for something greater than sport. Never allow your dedication to your sport to take the place of your devotion to God, your love for family, or your development as a human being. At the end of the day, your achievements in sport will never be more important than your achievements as a spouse, parent, or friend. You are a person first, an athlete second.

Rest.

You are not your own; you were
bought at a price. Therefore honor
God with your body.

—1 Corinthians 6:19-20

SELF-CARE

Athletes call it *burnout*. Sports physicians give it another name: *overtraining syndrome.* It is a condition in which an athlete experiences fatigue and diminished performance in spite of continuing— or even increasing—their training. The symptoms include mood changes, decreased motivation, frequent injuries, and infections. This condition results form the emotional and physical stress of prolonged training. The symptoms result from changes in hormones, physical fatigue, and the suppression of the immune system.

Oddly, the way that many athletes cope with burnout is to train even harder. Seeing a decline in their performance and motivation, they wrongly conclude that the best solution is to increase their level of training—thereby increasing the very stresses that have created burnout in the first place. What the body really needs to recover from burnout is something much more basic: rest.

Do not ignore your need for rest. This is the way God created you. His command is to take one day in seven for rest. When you rest properly, you free your mind from the stress of performance, allow your body to recover, and restore the competitive edge that you lose by overtraining. A proper training plan— and life plan—includes down time. Rest. Relax. Let go of the sport for a day. Your body will thank you.

Respect the sport.

You can't get much done in life if
you only work when you feel good.

—Jerry West

TEAMWORK

Everybody loves the game when things are going well—when your team is winning, when you're free of injury, when you're making great plays, when you feel invincible. At times like this you can't stop talking about it, thinking about it, and singing its praises. You love the sport, and you know it. The same is true in the game of life. When all is going your way, when the sun is shining down on you, it's easy to bless the name of the Lord.

It's when things aren't going so well that commitment wavers. You may even begin cursing the game, wishing you could quit. You look for a way out. In life, when the world's not as it should be, it might even be tempting to curse the name of the Lord, to quit trusting Him.

But you've got to respect the sport. You've got to let it play out. You've got to ride this wave with commitment and dedication, never letting your team down by giving up or giving in. In life, you've got to respect the journey God's put you on. You've got to keep going, hold your head up high, and trust that God will make something good of this.

Be unselfish.

A successful team beats

with one heart.

—Sarah Redmond

TEAMWORK

Knowing whether you are a ball hog is as easy, and as difficult, as knowing whether you are singing in tune. To hear yourself sing, all you need to do is replay a recording of yourself or watch the reaction of others. The hard part is taking the time to do it. Likewise, to figure out whether you are being selfish with the ball, all you have to do is watch yourself from the perspective of others; taking the time to discern whether you are being appropriate is the hard part. Most of us prefer to live in ignorance about our weaknesses.

Assessing yourself doesn't just take time, of course; it also requires you to be brutally honest with yourself. How much easier it is to justify your actions by thinking that your unwillingness to trust others with the ball is only because you are the stronger player, because you want to help the team. The truth is that the best way to help the team is to build such a level of trust that your work together with precision, no matter the skill level of the individual players.

Are you willing to put aside your personal desires for the sake of the team, on and off the court? Do you see yourself as someone special who deserves special treatment, or do you contribute all you have for the sake of the team, and sacrifice yourself for others when necessary? If it's the latter, then you have experienced the beauty of God's upside-down Kingdom, where the first shall be last and those who sacrifice have the greatest reward.

Have a plan.

The will to win is important,

but the will to prepare is vital.

—Joe Paterno

GOALS

No matter how fervently you believe Santa Claus is real, this fictional character will always remain a figment of our collective imagination. You can't will Santa into existence. Likewise, you can't win a game by sheer desire. You can talk smack to your opponents and even believe your own words, but wanting something isn't the same as achieving it. The desire to win, of course, is good—but only if it feeds your passion to train well. Go ahead and talk smack, but then get to the practice field so you won't need to eat crow.

No matter which sport you're doing—or which game of life you're playing—having a plan affects what you do and whether you achieve success. It's important to have the big goal of winning, but it's just as important to know the steps to achieving this goal. Imagine making big plans to go to Disney World with your family—even buying tickets to get in—without pulling out a map to figure out how to get there; you get on the road with emotions high, but no one has any idea how to get there, so you just drive hoping it will all work out.

Make a plan. Know how to get from where you are to where you want to be. And then follow the plan.

Fight through pain.

This is a tough game. There are times when you've got to play hurt, when you've got to block out the pain.

—Shaquille O'Neal

BRAVERY

Avoiding things we don't like is the primary preoccupation of our society. We have built all kinds of gadgets to help us to do that— from dishwashers to motorized vehicles to elevators. We hire people to do the work we want to avoid, and we believe the message that tells us we deserve the easy life. Advertisements promise big results with no effort, immediate results with little investment. No wonder working hard is so foreign to us.

Athletics may be the last stand against this culture's false sense of entitlement. In sports you can't pretend you deserve to win based on your good personality or the color of your skin or who your parents are. In sports you can't abuse the gift of grace by doing nothing and expecting everything. In sports you experience the direct correlation of hard work and results. You find the courage to dig deep, to face the pain, to press on because you know the reward.

Be willing to make the sacrifices that are required for success. Nobody will hand this one to you. You must earn it for yourself, and that will require hard work, physical courage, strength of will, and, yes, bravery. The good news? You've got this. You *can* do it. You have what it takes to win.

Discipline your mind.

Be positive and work hard. I think it's possible to overcome anything if you're willing to work at it.

—Sheryl Swoopes

HOPE

Sports movies seem to be everyone's favorites. We can't help but feel the emotional satisfaction of an underdog achieving victory after a long struggle with various conflicts. We love to celebrate the success of these sports heroes as if it's our own victory—because in a way it is. Hearing stories of hope propels us to press on, to overcome the things that threaten to get in our way of victory.

As an athlete, don't neglect to keep success stories in the forefront of your mind. Watch movies, read books, listen to personal stories—do what it takes to fill your mind with these words of hope so that you can press on when the task before you seems impossible. And encourage yourself with the knowledge that your hard work is inspiring someone else.

Don't just apply this concept to the game, of course. Let yourself embrace the beauty of hope for everysituation that comes before you. Consider the most powerful story of hope that Jesus Christ himself offers us: When all seemed lost Jesus sacrificed himself, died on the cross, and then rose victoriously from the grave to redeem all of mankind. Don't forget, Phil. 4:8 reminds believers that we should discipline our lives to think about doing what is right. Plus, the positivity of this verse brings hope to the disciplined life.

Don't believe the hype.

Before a downfall the heart
is haughty, but humility comes
before honor.

—Proverbs 18:12

HUMILITY

You're not all that and a bag of chips. You're no more important than anyone else. It doesn't matter how good you are at the sport you play, it doesn't matter how many people affirm you and thrill over your accomplishments, you're just a regular person. It's important to remember that not just so that you'll treat others with the respect and honor they deserve, but so that you will not fall victim to the tyranny of praise.

Without humility—without admiring God for the gift he gave you rather than admiring yourself—you are vulnerable. For now, while the spotlight is shining on you, you will not feel the pain of glory; you may not be aware that your haughtiness is eating your soul. But you are training yourself to live for the opinion of others; and later, when your body ages, your skills fade, and your fans disappear, you will feel the darkness. Without humility you cannot know the deep joy of acceptance that doesn't come from anything you do, but from who you are.

Work hard. Pursue success. Celebrate victory. But always turn your heart toward the One who is more important than yourself. When you receive praise, remember the One who is truly worthy of honor. Reflect your praise and glory up to God. He alone is worthy.

Know your limits.

A life is not important except in the
impact it has on other lives.

—Jackie Robinson

SELF-UNDERSTANDING

It's just a game, right? Why then do we care so much about winning? Why do we spend billions of dollars each year on athletics on all levels—professional, college, high school, recreational, junior? Why do we spend a high percentage of hours each week on watching or participating in sports? Maybe because it's not just a game. Sports affects athletes and spectators in profound ways.

It's important to understand what drives us to sports—what drives *you* to sports. Are you playing for the thrill of the game, to gain glory, to stay fit, to earn money, to enjoy the company of others, to relieve boredom, to provide inspiration to others? When you are aware of your purpose for working so hard to achieve success in the field of athletics, you will be able to keep a healthy perspective. You'll be able to keep things in balance rather than driving yourself to the point of physical or psychological harm.

Perhaps as you discern your motivation, you might even work towards changing your reason for participating in athletics. You can determine whether you are spending too much time or not enough time on the sport in terms of how it affects your team, your loved ones, your audience, and yourself.

Take it up a notch.

It is not the size of a man but the size of his heart that matters.

—Evander Holyfield

INTENSITY

Everyone knows it's not just physical strength or athletic skill that makes a person good at sports. A great athlete has guts. A great athlete has heart. If you are able to push yourself just a little bit further, a little bit longer, or a little bit faster—after you've hit what you thought was your limit—then you've discovered the phenomenon that transforms an athlete into a superstar.

God has created the human body to function with precision that far surpasses any computer we could create and with efficiency that surpasses the best car we could design. He has given us strength and skill, determination and drive. It's up to us to push ourselves to our maximum potential he has given us—and that potential is almost always far more than we imagine.

Increasing intensity is more about the mind than the body. It takes strength of heart and mind to keep going when it seems impossible to keep going. And always the reward is far greater than the physical accomplishment. We build self-esteem that transfers into all areas of our life, and we gain a respect for the One who created us—and an ability to trust Him when He calls us to do the impossible.

Persevere.

I have fought the good fight,

I have finished the race,

I have kept the faith.

—2 Timothy 4:7

FORTITUDE

Sometimes it requires a great deal of courage to follow our dreams. Writer Mark Walters relates the story of Earl J. Fleming, an Alaska biologist, who performed an incredibly dangerous experiment to investigate the bear's reputation for attacking humans. When Fleming encountered a bear, he neither ran away from it nor shot it. By the end of his study, he had encountered eighty-one brown bears. Although several of them staged mock attacks, not one actually attacked Walters.

Your pursuit of excellence may not be as terrifying as coming face to face with a wild bear, but you will certainly need fortitude if you are to reach your dreams. Opponents can be intimidating. The physical demands of the sport may be grueling. No success will come without dedication, perseverance, and courage. These traits are not developed in the comfort of the living room. In order to develop strength, you need to go into the very places that tax your abilities. Like the Alaska biologist, you must be willing to face the very things that threaten your success—your own limitations.

What is currently pushing you beyond your limits? Do you have the courage to face it? Keep going. Push beyond what you think you are capable of. Summon the courage to persevere. You can do this!

Be relentless.

It's not where you start out in life,

it's where you end up.

—Frank Leonard

TENACITY

Do not become discouraged when the results you'd like don't come easily or quickly. History is filled with examples of slow starters who went on to achieve great things. Winston Churchill seemed so dull as a youth that his father thought he might be incapable of earning a living. Thomas Edison's first teacher described him as addled. Albert Einstein's parents feared their child was dull, and he performed so badly in all high school courses except mathematics that a teacher asked him to drop out.

In order to achieve any goal, you must be willing to take risks, venture forward, and keep going. Fainthearted souls never do well in the field of sport. Victory depends on determination, doggedness, persistence—the sheer will to keep going when every fiber of your being would rather quit.

What tempts you to abandon your dreams? When are you most vulnerable to the temptation to quit. Remember that nothing worth doing can be achieved quickly or easily. You can achieve more than you thought possible for yourself if you can simply be patient, keep going, and don't give up.

Have the will to survive.

Resolve never to quit, never to give up, no matter what the situation.

—Jack Nicklaus

RELENTLESSNESS

Distance runner Marla Runyon, legally blind for twenty-two years, competed in the 2000 Summer Olympic Games in Sydney, Australia, where she qualified for the finals in the 1,500-meter race and finished in eighth place. According to a September 22, 2000, report on the *Today Show*, Runyon can't see in color. She sees only a fuzzy blob. During races, she simply follows the blob of figures in front of her. Her real challenge comes after rounding the last curve, where she must sprint in front of others. Runyon courageously forges ahead, however, in spite of her inability to see the finish line. She says, "I just know where it is."

Every athlete must have the will to survive in order to compete. Like Runyon, everyone faces some obstacle. Some have physical attributes that are challenging. Others carry emotional, psychological, or spiritual baggage that makes them believe they are not good enough or cannot win. No one comes to the competition in perfect shape. We all have something to overcome. Winning—or even finishing—requires the willingness to forge ahead, swallow the fear, take the pain, and persevere.

When you hit the wall—physically or mentally— keep going. Do not allow your limitations to define you. Keep working. Keep moving. Keep growing. Keep going. Never, never, never give up.

Follow the rules.

It is better to be defeated on principle than to win on lies.

—Arthur Calwell

INTEGRITY

According to a January 10, 2001, story in the Chicago Tribune, Mark Cuban, owner of the NBA's Dallas Mavericks, once offered WGN Chicago Radio sports-talk host David Kaplan $50,000 to change his name legally to "Dallas Maverick." When Kaplan declined, Cuban offered to pay Kaplan $100,000 and donate $100,000 to Kaplan's favorite charity if he would take the name for just one year. In spite of the urging of many listeners, Kaplan resolutely refused the offer. He said, "I'd be saying I'd do anything for money, and that bothers me. My name is my birthright. I'd like to preserve my integrity and credibility."

At some point you will face the challenge to compromise your principles for the advancement of your athletic career. The challenge may come when you realize that you can enhance your performance using drugs rather than discipline. Or it may be that you will be tempted to sacrifice your relationship or your word for the sake of an opportunity.

Resist the urge to win at the expense of yourself. Your integrity is your most precious possession. Prize it above any achievement—on or off the athletic field. You have only one name, one life, and one soul. Guard them well.

Give yourself to others.

Individual commitment to
a group effort—that is what
makes a team work.

—Vince Lombardi

SELFLESSNESS

We could learn a lesson in teamwork from an unusual teacher—the honeybee. On a warm day about half the bees in a hive stay inside beating their wings while the other half go out to gather pollen and nectar. Because of the beating wings, the temperature inside the hive is about ten degrees cooler than outside. The bees rotate duties so that the bees who cool the hive one day go out to gather honey the next. Every drop of honey that you've ever consumed has been the product of an amazing team of bees, each with their own role to play.

It may sound simplistic, but the old adage really is true. The meaning of *team* is Together Everyone Accomplishes More. When you are able to place your need for recognition in subordination to the good of the team, you are far more likely to be successful. When each member believes that his or her teammates would gladly sacrifice themselves for the team, the entire unit grows stronger. When we specialize on our strengths and allow others to cover our weaknesses, the sum of our effort becomes greater than any one part.

It is one of life's best-kept secrets that there is more joy in giving than in receiving. When you discover the thrill of helping others achieve their full potential, you are far more likely to experience success yourself. Don't be afraid to give yourself away.

Learn from failure.

You will be who you are

becoming right now.

—John C. Maxwell

GROWTH

Pastor Mark Batterson, in the book *In a Pit with a Lion on a Snowy Day*, tells of a visit to the doctor to have his allergies treated. Much to Batterson's surprise, the treatment did not consist of finding ways to alleviate his symptoms. Instead, his doctor pricked his forearm in eighteen places to inject tiny amounts of different allergens. The point was not simply to avoid the things that cause an adverse reaction but to *identify* them so that a cure could be found. There is a profound point here about learning from failure. Batterson writes, "The cure for fear of failure is not success; it's failure. The cure for fear of rejection is not acceptance; it's rejection. You have to be exposed to small quantities of whatever you're afraid of. That's how you build up immunity to fear."

You will make progress in your sport and in your life only to the degree that you are able to face your fears, learn from your failures, and move confidently into the future. It is impossible to achieve victory with no failures, no setbacks, no disappointments. Mistakes are inevitable. What matters is how you respond to them, whether you learn from them, and what you do the next time out on the field.

Have you failed recently? Perfect. You're in an ideal position to grow.

Enjoy the game.

People will tell you that I overcame obstacles? Maybe. But the truth is I was incredibly blessed in my life. More was given than was ever taken away.

—Jim Abbott

PLEASURE

Pope John Paul II was the spiritual leader to millions. Later in his life, he reflected on his journey: "After I had faith, living things became precious to me. I wanted to pet them, hug them—babies and dogs and lizards, whatever. For me the great fruit of belief is joy. There is a God, there is a purpose, there is a meaning to things, there are realities we cannot guess at, there is a big peace, and you are part of it."

Enjoying sport—just like enjoying life—depends on taking an occasional time out to enjoy the journey. When you spend all of your time working, training, and competing, the sport itself can lose its luster. You may lose the childlike thrill of hitting the ball, riding the bike, or diving into the pool.

Don't allow it! Take time to enjoy the little things that you once looked forward to—putting on the helmet or stepping onto the court, the bounce of a fresh ball on your racquet or the smell of new gloves. Enjoy the green grass, the blue water, and the white chalk lines. Sport was meant to be enjoyed as well as won. Don't forget the former, even while you strive for the latter. Go ahead, smell the roses. It's a great day to be alive!

Chart your growth.

You can practice shooting eight hours a day, but if your technique is wrong, then all you become is very good at shooting the wrong way.

—Michael Jordan

PROGRESS

When the great musician Pablo Casals reached the age of ninety-five, a young reported asked him this question: "Mr. Casals, you are ninety-five and the greatest cellist that ever lived. Why do you still practice six hours a day?" Casals answered, "Because I think I'm making progress."

Your goal should be to make progress every day of your life. Most of the time, that progress will be difficult to see. Just as you never actually see the grass grow or the tide come in, you may have difficulty seeing the progress that you are making in strength, conditioning, or technique. You may undertake the same workouts day after day or week after week and feel that you are getting nowhere. It may be tempting to conclude that you are not progressing at all.

That's why it is important to chart your progress. You need a "mirror" that can be held up before you from time to time and give you a visual reminder of how far you have come. Record your lap times. Track your weight gain or loss. Measure the distance you walk, run, swim, ride, or throw. Know what your completion percentage is. These personal stats will never tell you how well you have done versus the competition, but they will tell you how well you are doing against yourself. Look how far you've come!

Forget yesterday.

Every day is a new opportunity.
You can build on yesterday's
success or put its failures behind
and start over again.

—Bob Feller

RESILIENCE

There may be thirty days in a month and seven days in a week, but there are only three days that matter to any person: yesterday, today, and tomorrow. Most people choose one of those days to be the focus of their attention. The day that they choose speaks volumes about their outlook—and their potential.

Yesterday is the day of remembrance and regret. Those who focus on yesterday choose to live in the past. Those who have been successful tend to live on their memories. They think more about what they have done than about what they are doing. Or they may be consumed by regret, believing that no real achievement is possible in the future.

Tomorrow is a better choice for one's focus, but there are pitfalls with this option as well. Those who look exclusively at tomorrow may become idealistic, always dreaming about what might be rather than what is. Tomorrow is a day for hope, but not necessarily for action.

Today is the day that brings results. Today is when we can act, think, move, change, or grow. Yesterday, with both its triumphs and failures, is past. Close the box and put it away. Tomorrow may never come. Do not expend so much time or energy dreaming of things that will be that you neglect the things that are. Live today. Work today. Train today. This is your day.

Encourage
teammates.

Leadership is a matter of having people
look at you and gain confidence, seeing
how you react. If you're in control,
they're in control.

—Tom Landry

SOLIDARITY

Author Larry Crabb relates that when he was a young person, those in his church were expected to pray aloud in Communion services. This was a huge problem for the young man, who suffered from stuttering. He recalls that after offering what seemed to be a very confused prayer that rambled quite a bit, he felt defeated and discouraged. He vowed to himself that he would never again pray in front of a group. But at the close of the service, an older man stopped him by the door and said, "Larry, there's one thing I want you to know. Whatever you do for the Lord, I'm behind you 1,000 percent." Larry Crabb went on to become a highly successful author and speaker. In his book *Encouragement,* Crabb writes, "Those words were life words. They had power. They reached deep into my being."

You have that same power to lift up your teammates, coworkers, training partners, and family members. You can unleash the power of encouragement in the lives of others. Your words can build others up, give them confidence, and restore broken pride and bruised feelings. The words you say to others can be words of life to them.

Who needs a word of encouragement today? Which of your associates is struggling with self-esteem or overcoming grief or facing disappointment? Speak words of life to them today.

Have a game plan.

Setting a goal is not the main thing.
It is deciding how you will go
about achieving it and
staying with that plan.

—Knute Rockne

KNOWLEDGE

If the world's knowledge were represented graphically, the total amount of learning from the beginning of recorded history up to 1845 would rise to the height of about one inch. From 1845 to 1945 would build the tower another three inches in height. And the amount of knowledge available from 1945 to the present would rise to the height of the Washington Monument! We live in a world driven by information. It is impossible to succeed in any business or profession without mastering the knowledge of that field.

Learning also plays an important role in athletic achievement. Athletics is not a physical pursuit only; it involves the mind. The limits of the body can be reached more fully when a safe, sensible training regimen is used. Understanding how proper diet strengthens the body helps the athlete achieve and maintain peak performance. Knowing the opponent's strengths and weaknesses is vital for success.

Where are the gaps in your sports knowledge? What do you not know that you need to know in order to grow stronger, train more effectively, or race more competitively? And how will you acquire that knowledge? What is your game plan for increasing your learning? As you are building your body, don't neglect to strengthen your mind.

Believe.

Confidence is contagious.

So is lack of confidence.

—Vince Lombardi

FAITH

In his book *A Coach's Story*, NFL legend John McKay tells a story illustrating the supreme confidence of University of Alabama football coach Bear Bryant: "We were out shooting ducks, and finally, after about three hours, here comes one lonely duck. The Bear fires. And that duck is still flying today. But Bear watched the duck flap away, looked at me and said, 'John, you are witnessing a genuine miracle. There flies a dead duck!'"

Faith is a vital ingredient for achievement in sport. This goes beyond mere self-confidence, brashness, or the braggadocio that is all too common in athletics. Faith is the willingness to believe in what cannot be seen or proven. Faith is believing that you can complete a marathon, even though you have failed on a previous attempt. Faith is the willingness to believe that the odds makers don't have the power to determine the outcome of your game. Faith is knowing that you can prevail in spite of the fact that the opponent is stronger and more experienced. Faith is the unseen power that fuels every winner.

If you lack faith, begin at the beginning. There is a God who created you and who loves you. Believe in Him, commit yourself to Him. And believe in yourself. God believes in you.

Be a positive leader.

Nothing can stop the man with the right mental attitude from achieving his goal; nothing on earth can help the man with the wrong mental attitude.

—Thomas Jefferson

OUTLOOK

Exceptional winning streaks by teams at relatively obscure high schools or colleges are not uncommon, but it was interesting when *Sports Illustrated* reported that the girls volleyball team at Dayville High School in Oregon had a streak of sixty-five victories before losing a match. The streak wouldn't have been quite so impressive except that the school had only eighteen girl students, sixteen of whom were on the volleyball team. Although one of the smallest Class B schools in the state, Dayville won the Class A volleyball championship three years in a row. Part of its success was due to the team's positive outlook. It is reported that the letter that announced the winning streak said that after the defeat, "The team rebounded and has a winning streak of one."

Your mental attitude is every bit as important to your athletic success as is your physical strength. When your outlook is good, there is no obstacle to high and no challenge too great. Conversely, when your attitude is one of discouragement, disillusionment, or disappointment, defeat is certain to follow. You may not be able to achieve all that you think you can, but you certainly will not achieve what you believe you can't.

What is possible for you today? What barriers will you break? What victories will you achieve? That all depends on your attitude.

Be self-motivated.

The ones who want to achieve
and win championships
motivate themselves.

—Mike Ditka

DISCIPLINE

It has been said that when the greatpiano virtuoso Ignace Jan Paderewsky played before Queen Victoria, she was greatly impressed by his skill. "Mr. Paderewsky," she exclaimed, "you are a genius."Paderewsky demurred. "Perhaps, Your Majesty," he said, "but before that I was a drudge." He was referring to the number of hours that he spent practicing every day. Whoever said that creativity is 1 percent inspiration and 99 percent perspiration might as easily have been talking about athletics. The stunning one-handed catch, the breath-taking toe-loop, and the seemingly effortless three-point shot all have this in common: they require hours upon hours of disciplined practice.

Talent is not enough. The greatest talents, without discipline, are mere has-beens and also-rans. Natural ability is the raw material of sport. Discipline is the hammer that pounds it into something useful.

What is the point at which you are tempted to back off on your physical training or skill practice? What is the drill that you would like to omit or the workout that you would skip if you could? If you are able to discipline yourself to train when no one is forcing you, complete the reps when no one is watching, and give 100 percent effort even when you are exhausted, you will be rewarded with increased performance—and greater self-respect.

Use the pain.

Courage is not the absence of fear,
but simply moving on with dignity
despite that fear.

—Pat Riley

COURAGE

Radio commentator Paul Harvey tells the story of Ray Blankenship, who looked up from the breakfast table one morning to see a small girl being swept along in the rain-flooded drainage ditch beside his Andover, Ohio, home. Without hesitation, Blankenship ran out the door and raced along the ditch, trying to get ahead of the child. Finally, he hurled himself into the churning waters, grasping the girl by the arm. They were swept along by the current and were about to be forced down a drainage culvert when Ray's hand found something firm to hold on to. "If I can just hang on until help comes," he thought. Within a few more minutes, he was able to pull the girl to safety. Rescue workers treated both of them for shock. And on April 12, 1989, Ray Blankenship was awarded the Coast Guard's Silver Lifesaving Medal. And here is the truly amazing part of the story—Ray Blankenship can't swim.

Courage is the willingness to face immediate risk for a greater goal. Courage is what enables a 185-pound running back to hurl himself into a wall of 300-pound defensive linemen. Courage is what drives a distance runner mile after mile, in spite of the searing pain in lungs and limbs. Courage is what propels a high diver back up the ladder after a painful entry. Courage is a requirement for success in any sport at any position at any time.

Are you facing a difficult challenge today? Take courage. You can compete, you can endure, you can win.

Take risks.

If what you did yesterday seems big,
you haven't done anything today.

—Lou Holtz

CHALLENGE

In his book, *Living about the Level of Mediocrity,* Chuck Swindoll tells of meeting a man who had served on one of Walt Disney's original advisory boards. Those early days were difficult, but Disney had a remarkable, creative vision, and he refused to quit. Walt would occasionally present some unbelievable, extensive dream he was entertaining. Usually, the members of his board would stare back in disbelief, resisting even the thought of taking such a large risk. Here's what's fascinating: unless every member resisted the idea, Disney usually didn't pursue it. He figured that the challenge wasn't big enough to merit his time and energy unless his board was completely intimidated by it!

If you are going to make progress as an athlete, coach, or team, you must be wiling to take some risks. If you only enter races that you know you can finish in the top ten, you'll never be pushed to your full potential. If you never attempt an achievement that you are unsure you can master, you will never grow. If all you are willing to do is all that you have ever done, then all you will ever be is what you are.

Dare to dream. Dare to risk. Dare to grow. That is the only way to find out how good you can truly be!

Celebrate victory.

Enjoying success requires the
ability to adapt. Only by being
open to change will you have
a true opportunity to get the
most from your talent.

—Nolan Ryan

REWARD

It has been estimated that a man laughs, on average, sixty-nine times a day, and a woman laughs fifty-five times. It is uncertain what accounts for the discrepancy, but this much is certain: people who have learned to laugh lead healthier, happier lives. It is important to take a break from the hard work of, well, hard work occasionally and enjoy the moment. Laughter, moments of light-hearted camaraderie, and just plain celebrating the good times are vital for success in any endeavor. When you take time to celebrate the small wins, you help ensure that you will be around to celebrate the big ones.

The temptation is to keep your nose so firmly pressed to the grindstone that you fail to notice the progress toward your overall goal. Mindful that one win doesn't make a season, you press immediately into the next week's practice schedule without taking time to congratulate your teammates. Or you become so focused on the physical conditioning you have left to achieve that you don't take satisfaction in the progress already made.

Determine to acknowledge every victory, even the small ones. Notice the progress you are making as an athlete or as a team. Congratulate your teammates or training partners on their gains. Enjoy the journey, even though you may have a long way yet to go. When you have reached a goal, celebrate!

Don't gloat.

A team is where a boy can prove his courage on his own. A gang is where a coward goes to hide.

—Mickey Mantle

RESPECT

George Whitefield and John Wesley were the two best-known preachers of the eighteenth century. Thought they knew each other well, they had a significant theological disagreement. One day someone asked Whitefield if he thought he would see Wesley in heaven. It was the perfect opportunity to lob a verbal missile at his theological opponent. But Whitefield did just the opposite. He said, "I fear not, for he will be so near the eternal throne and we, at such a distance, we shall hardly get sight of him."

Athletics is based on competition, and some rivalries can become bitter. At some point you will be tempted to gloat over a hard-earned victory or belittle a difficult opponent. Talking smack may seem like a way to vent frustration or gain satisfaction over an opponent who may have competed unfairly, but it reflects more on the speaker than on the object. When you belittle your opponent, you belittle yourself.

Resist the temptation to disparage your opponent. Remember that grace is always more attractive than pride, and there is no profit in tearing others down—even when they have insulted you. Never resort to taunts, insults, or cheap shots. You're better than that.

Be mentally tough.

Athletic competition clearly defines

the unique power of our attitude.

—Bart Starr

ATTITUDE

The apostle Paul knew what it was to face challenges. This plucky defender of the faith was once shipwrecked, he spent a day and night on the open sea, he was hunted like a criminal and falsely imprisoned, beaten, and the object of a murder plot. Yet he became one of the most prolific missionaries in the history of Christianity and contributed many of the letters that comprise the New Testament. Near the end of his life, he wrote these amazing words: "I know what it is to be in need, and I know what it is to have plenty. I have learned the secret of being content in any and every situation, whether well fed or hungry, whether living in plenty or in want. I can do all this through Him who gives me strength" (Philippians 4:12–13).

You, too, can have an attitude of optimism and faith in spite of the challenges that you are facing. Through faith in Christ, you can not just endure but overcome every obstacle. Your faith is not a secret weapon for victory in athletic competition, but it is the foundation of a positive mental attitude that will help you achieve in every area of your life.

When you are tempted to quit, and you will be, hang tough! When you face challenges from competitors or coworkers, keep a positive attitude. You can do all things through Christ, who gives you strength.

Respect yourself.

If your goal is to be average, you will almost always come up short.

—Bill Bajema

SELF-ESTEEM

In her book *Let Me Be a Woman,* Elizabeth Elliot tells the story of Gladys Aylward, who was dissatisfied with the body God had given to her. While all of Gladys's friends seemed to be tall with beautiful blond hair, she was just four feet ten inches tall and had dark hair. Always feeling a bit out of place, Gladys decided to become a missionary. When she arrived in the country where she was to serve, she stood on the wharf in Shanghai and looked around at the people to whom she would minister. "Every one of them had black hair," she said, "and every one of them had stopped growing when I did."

God knew what he was doing when he created you. In spite of your physical limitations or flaws, you are a uniquely crafted individual. Your life has value. You matter to God, and you should matter to yourself as well.

Never allow your physical traits, past experiences, hurts, or failures to diminish your sense of worth. Remember that nobody can take advantage of your without your permission. No one can disrespect you unless you let them. It is impossible for anyone to humiliate you unless you grant them that privilege. You have the ability to control who gets inside your head. Respect yourself. You are worth it!

Give yourself to the game.

Being the best that you can
be is possible only if your desire
to be a champion is greater than
your fear of failure.

—Sammy Lee

ABANDONMENT

The great artist Michelangelo was just fourteen years old when he began studying with the art master Bertoldo de Giovanni. Even so, the teacher could recognize the tremendous potential of his young student. Yet the old man realized that great talents can sometimes be tempted to rely on their natural abilities rather than develop to their true potential. They need accountability in order to grow. One day Bertoldo entered the studio find Michelangelo toying with a sculpture that was far beneath his abilities. Without hesitation Bertoldo took a hammer and smashed the work into tiny pieces, shouting, "Talent is cheap! Dedication is costly!"

If you will develop your true potential, you must dedicate yourself to your sport. It will take time, energy, mental focus, and a great deal of commitment. It is tempting to settle for less than your best, relying on the results you have already achieved. You may already be good enough to beat 90 percent of the competition. To win against the best will take more than you have already given.

What is holding you back from achieving your true potential? Are your limits external—or are they within you? What are you willing to surrender in order to achieve your goals? In sport, as in your spiritual life, there is no growth without sacrifice.

Learn to improvise.

Everyone has a plan 'til they get
punched in the mouth.

—Mike Tyson

ADAPTABILITY

Once there was a French nun who went door-to-door soliciting donations to help care for elderly people. She approached the home of a wealthy man who said he would donate 1,000 francs if she would have a glass of champagne with him. What a dilemma! It would clearly be improper to have a drink with this gentleman, but the sister also thought of the number of poor people who could be helped with such a large donation. She decided to accept. A servant brought in a bottle and poured a glass of champagne, and the little nun emptied it. Then she said, "That was excellent. I'll have another glass at the same price." And she got it!

Sometimes you must be willing to adapt in order to be successful. There are far too many variables in sport to believe that you can win the contest before you leave the locker room. Every athlete must be flexible, both physically and mentally.

The problem is that many of us are resistant to change. We keep the same workout routine even when results taper off. We stick with the game plan that worked last week, even though the opponent has changed. What unforeseen problem is affecting your performance—on or off the field? And here is the critical question: what changes can you make in order to thrive in this new environment?

Imagine the win.

The man who has no
imagination has no wings.

—Muhammad Ali

VISUALIZATION

The saying, "you've got to see it to believe it" is an age old statement about the power of visualization. Simply put, visualization is the mental exercise of picturing in your mind the ideal state or condition that you hope to recreate in life. In the spiritual life, you may visualize yourself displaying virtues in a real-life setting, such as being patient with your children during a stressful car trip or being self-controlled when challenged at a business meeting by a difficult coworker. The practice of seeing yourself in those settings can have a powerful effect on your future behavior.

The same is true of your sports performance. Many athletes have difficulty believing that they *can* win. Though they desire the top spot with all their hearts, they have an internal block that keeps them from achieving. They fear that they will lack courage in the critical moment, drop the ball on a key play, or fail to persevere at the end of the race.

If you are to achieve, you must believe that you can. So go ahead, close your eyes and imagine your next competitive event. How do you hope you will perform? Imagine it. See it. Believe it. That is your team, working together flawlessly. That's you, edging out the competition at the line. You can do it, and you will.

Define success.

Do you not know that in a race
all the runners run, but only one
gets the prize? Run in such a
way as to get the prize.

—1 Corinthians 9:24

OWNERSHIP

It is said that when Queen Victoria was a child, she didn't know she was in line for the throne of England. Her instructors, trying to prepare her for the future, were frustrated because they couldn't motivate her. She just didn't take her studies seriously. Finally, her teachers decided to tell her that one day she would become the queen of England. Upon hearing this, Victoria quietly said, "Then I will be good." The realization that she had inherited this high calling gave her a sense of responsibility that profoundly affected her conduct from then on.

You will be successful only when you take responsibility for your own results. As long as you envision your coaches, your teammates, the officials, or even the weather as determining your success or failure on the field, you will never reach your full potential. It will always be too easy to blame others for any failures and insulate yourself from the consequences of your choices. To achieve, you must determine to own the results.

What does success look like to you? What is your definition of failure? What will you do to put yourself in a position to win? Who will be responsible if you fail? When you have clear answers to those questions, you are in a position to achieve. When you are able to say, "If it is to be, it is up to me," you are ready for victory.

Have courage.

In life, as in a football game,

the principle to follow is:

Hit the line hard.

—Theodore Roosevelt

TOUGHNESS

In August of the year 480 B.C., King Leonidas was set to lead his tiny force of three hundred Spartans against the vast Persian army. The emperor sent an envoy to Leonidas, urging surrender. The messenger explained that resistance would be futile in the face of such an overwhelming force. "Our archers are so numerous," he said, "that the flight of their arrows will darken the sun."

"So much the better," Leonidas replied, "for we shall fight in the shade." Leonidas and his gallant three hundred made their stand at the Battle of Thermopylae, killing some twenty thousand of the enemy before he died in battle.

Courage is as much about attitude as about physical vigor. To face any enemy, let alone one with superior force, the athlete must have the mental toughness to take on risk, challenge, and even pain without blinking. It requires an mind-set that says, "I will give it my all, whatever the cost." That same attitude is necessary for success as a parent, marriage partner, entrepreneur, or community leader. You must be willing to risk, willing to endure, willing to lose if you are ever to win.

What holds you back from being mentally tough? What are you most afraid of losing? Time? Money? Pride? Self-respect? When you are willing to risk all you are in a position to win all. Take courage. You cannot win without it.

Listen to your body.

Troubles are only mental;

it is the mind that manufactures

them, and the mind can gorge them,

banish them, abolish them.

—Mark Twain

AWARENESS

Rick and Michelle are a married couple who couldn't be more opposite. He is the strong silent type. She is Ms. Personality, always enjoying a conversation. "It's not that Rick doesn't listen," Michelle complained, "he just doesn't listen to *me*." It seems that she had spent about half an hour explaining to her husband the plans she had for decorating their home for Christmas. She described her elaborate vision, complete with angels and reindeer. Moments later, Rick looked up from his magazine and said, "Hey Honey, do realize it's almost Thanksgiving. We need to think about getting a Christmas tree."

Some athletes have even less awareness than Rick. Signs of impending injury or poor performance are all around them, but the fail to pick up on them. They ignore persistent soreness that is the precursor of a muscle strain. They fight thorugh fatigue rather than recognizing the symptom of over-training. It isn't that they don't pay attention—they just don't pay attention to themselves.

Socrates advised, "Know thyself," and it's good advice for athletes. What are the signals that you are close to your physical limits? How much stress can you handle before you develop physical symptoms? What does your body need to recover from a hard workout? Listen to your body. Stay in tune with your mental, physical, and spiritual condition. If you don't care for yourself, who will?

Respect your opponent.

You can motivate by fear, and you can motivate by reward. But both of these methods are only temporary. The only lasting thing is self motivation.

—Homer Rice

PRINCIPLES

During wartime each side usually attempts to vilify the other. Masters of propaganda produce posters, sound bytes, and movie plots that cast the enemy as cowardly, villainous, and cruel. They invent derisive nicknames that dehumanize those fighting on the other side. Psychologically, this allows the hostiles to engage in mortal combat. Before you can destroy your enemy, you must be convinced that he or she deserves death.

On the field of competition, athletes sometimes employ a similar strategy to allow them to compete without mercy. Resist the temptation to disrespect or dehumanize your opponents. If you disrespect them, it will be easier to lower your own standards for competition by bending the rules, cheating, taking cheap shots, or even deliberately causing injury. By doing so you will cheapen both the game and any victory you might win. You will also cheapen yourself.

Respect the game, respect the rules, and respect your fellow competitors. Do not seek unfair advantages. Never allow frustration or fatigue get the better of you. Speak in respectful terms of your opponents, win or lose. Make a distinction between criticizing their tactics or performance and criticizing the people behind them. Treat others as you would like to be treated, on and off the field. There is no way to lose doing what is right.

Find a partner.

As iron sharpens iron, so one person

sharpens another.

—Proverbs 27:17

CAMARADERIE

Jesse Owens was the favorite in the long jump at the 1936 games in Berlin. His previous best jump of over 26 feet 8 inches set a record that would stand for a quarter century. Yet the African American young man was nervous about competing in the capital of the Nazi regime, who believed that their race was superior to his. Prior to the qualifying jump, a tall, blond-haired German athlete introduced himself to Owens. Luz Long said, "You should be able to qualify with your eyes closed!" The two chatted in a friendly way, and Owens went on to win the event, one of four gold medals he earned in those games. Afterward, Luz Long was the first to congratulate Owens on his success.

Sport has a way of breaking down the barriers that exist between people. Competitors come to respect one another in spite of their difference. Enemies on the field can become friends when the final gun sounds. When we exert ourselves together, striving together—or even against one another—the bonds of friendship can be formed that will last a lifetime.

Who is your partner in training? What group of guys or gals keep you accountable to workout? If you have not discovered the joy and benefit of having a friend and partner in your sport, seek one. It will enrich both your training and your life.

Look down the road.

Even if you're on the right track,

you'll get run over if you just sit there.

—Will Rogers

PERCEPTION

"I was born with one bad eye." That's how my friend Jeff describes his problem with depth perception. "I can see all right, but I have difficulty judging the distance between objects." Fortunately, his new vehicle has both a rearview camera and built-in sonar that alerts him when he is within three feet of an object. "If not for that," he laughs, "I'd be running into things right and left!"

Many of us have a similar problem with perception with regard to our lives. We have difficulty judging what's down the road. We fail to realize when we have come too close to dangerous objects such as temptation, failure, or compromise. We also have trouble knowing just how close we are to success. Though we may be headed in the right direction, we have difficulty judging our progress.

If you are going to be successful as an athlete and as a child of God, you must learn to judge what matters most in life. Sharpen your depth perception by sticking close to the Word of God. Let Scripture be your sonar device, alerting you to both the dangers and blessings in life. Cultivate your awareness of God's truth by prayer and meditation. Hide the Word of God in your heart, and it will guide you home.

Live for more than sport.

Whatever you do, work at it with all your heart, as working for the LORD, not for human masters.

—Colossians 3:23

ETERNITY

One of the great moments in golf history
occurred when a Scotsman attempted to
teach the game to President Ulysses S. Grant. The tutor
placed a ball on the tee and took a big backswing, but
then missed the ball spraying dirt and grass all over the
commander in chief. The golfer tried second time and
then a third with the same result. After Grant had
observed a half-dozen attempts, he wryly observed,
"There seems to be a fair amount of exercise in this
game, but I fail to see the purpose of the ball."

Without a purpose, your efforts in sport will be
as meaningless as that golfer's missed swings.
Simply winning is not enough to make your efforts
meaningful. You must have some larger reason for
playing the game, otherwise you will be left feeling
empty and useless in spite of any awards you may
achieve.

What counts for purpose? Here are a few noble
reasons for taking up a sport: to learn discipline, to
improve your health, to sharpen your physical skills, to
teach others, to inspire achievement, to enrich the lives
of others, to teach values, to leave a legacy. Before you
head for your next workout or sign up for another
season, ask yourself this question: "Why am I doing
this?" When the answer is something larger than
yourself, you will already have received a reward.

See the future.

You have to expect things of yourself

before you can do them.

—Michael Jordan

VISION

John III Sobieski, king of Poland in the late 17th century, is remembered as the man who saved central Europe from invading armies of Turks in 1683. With the Turks at the walls of Vienna, Sobieski led a charge that broke the siege. His rescue of Vienna is considered one of the decisive battles in European history.

In announcing his great victory the king paraphrased the famous words of Caesar by saying simply, "I came; I saw; God conquered."

Achieving greatness in any arena requires a blend of hubris and humility. You must have both the vision and self-confidence to see a grand thing and purpose to do it. And you must also have the wisdom to realize that unless God empowers your pursuit, it will not succeed.

What do you envision doing in your arena of competition? It may be something as simple as completing a half-marathon—not winning, just finishing. Or your vision may be larger: to win your conference championship, to earn a podium spot at a major competition, to conquer a fourteen-thousand-foot climb. Whatever you hope to accomplish, you must first have the vision to see the possibility and the confidence to take the first step.

What do you envision achieving in your chosen field of sport? And what steps will you take to make that vision a reality?

Be committed.

Commit to the LORD whatever you do, and he will establish your plans.

—Proverbs 16:3

HONOR

When Julius Caesar landed on the shores of Britain with his Roman legions, he took a bold and decisive step to ensure the success of his military venture. Ordering his men to march to the edge of the Cliffs of Dover, he commanded them to look down at the water below. To their amazement, they saw every ship in which they had crossed the channel engulfed in flames. Caesar had deliberately cut off any possibility of retreat. Now that his soldiers were unable to return to the continent, there was nothing left for them to do but to advance and conquer. That is exactly what they did.

There is no substitute for commitment. It is what drives us to be our best, push beyond our limits, and achieve more than we think ourselves capable of. Those who lack commitment will pull up when the pain becomes intense. They will slack off when nobody is watching their workout. Or they will break their word to teammates—or to family members, coworkers, or friends. Commitment and honor go hand in hand.

If you are to succeed in your sport, you must go all in. Commit yourself fully to what you are doing. Set goals for yourself. Consider them carefully, take the counsel of friends, and pray about them. Then commit yourself to achieving them, and don't look back.

Compete to win.

For the Spirit God gave us does not
make us timid, but gives us power,
love and self-discipline.

—2 Timothy 1:7

DETERMINATION

Gail Devers was clearly in the lead during the 100-meter hurdles event in the 1992 Summer Olympic Games. Victory seemed certain for the young American sprinter. Unaccountably, she tripped over the final hurdle, the last obstacle to victory. Clearly in agony, she dragged herself to her knees and crawled the last five meters to the finish line. She finished fifth. During those same games, British runner Derek Redmond tore a hamstring during the 400 meter semifinal. He hobbled toward the line, determined to complete the race. His father ran from the stands to help him off the track, but Redmond would not abandon the race. Leaning on his father, he limped to the line while the crowd cheered his bravery and determination.

Nobody said that competition would be easy. The same goes for parenting, marriage, friendship, earning a living—or just plain being human. It takes determination to make the finish line. If you are going to run the race, determine to do you best, determine to finish, determine to win. You will face obstacles and failures, some of them agonizingly painful. Just remember, there is no prize for starting the race. The accolades come for finishing.

What tempts you to abandon the race? Ignore it. Avoid it. Or just plain outrun it. To succeed in sport, you must be determined to win.

Enjoy the struggle.

There has never been a great athlete
who died not knowing what pain is.

—Bill Bradley

JOY

John F. Kennedy appeared to be a dynamic young man when elected President of the United States in 1960. Yet the young President suffered from Addison's disease, a chronic condition that produces fatigue, muscle weakness, and pain. Kennedy often used crutches when not in public view, and he suffered from chronic pain. Billy Sutton, one of Kennedy's campaign aides said, "Yeah, he knew what pain was all about—had it. He wore this brace and the pain was always with him. It was like a friend. It never left him, pain."

The presence of pain does not indicate an absence of vigor, enthusiasm, or joy. It is possible to both experience pain and achieve victory. Labor and victory are not opposites. You can enjoy the journey even when it is difficult.

The days of your life are a precious gift, every one of them. Do not surrender any of them—not a single one—to depression, anger, frustration, or despair. Even when you are battling an injury, fighting an illness, enduring a tough workout, or being ridden by a tough coach, enjoy the day that God has given to you. It will not come again!

Tap your inner strength.

If you can believe it,

the mind can achieve it.

—Ronnie Lott

POWER

The Hoover Dam, located in Clark County, Nevada, is one of the technological wonders of the world. Its massive, 726-foot-high concrete wall holds back the Colorado River, harnessing the water flow for power generation. The rushing waters achieve speeds of eighty-five miles per hour and produce 4.2 billion kilowatt hours of electricity annually. Yet the surface of the water reservoir is placid, and the river flows smoothly from the foot of the dam. That's because all of the power is internal. The real work of the dam is far below the surface, unseen by the casual observer.

The same is true for you as a human being and as an athlete. Your greatest source of power is not seen in your muscle tone or skeletal strength. Your greatest power is within you—God at work within your spirit. The apostle Paul asks, "Do you not know that your body is a temple of the Holy Spirit, who is in you, whom you have received from God?" (1 Corinthians 6:19). It is this inner source of strength that will enable you to reach far beyond what your body alone is capable of doing.

Do no rely on your physical strength alone. You need the power of God within you in order to achieve—in sports or in life. Be in touch with God through His Word and through prayer. Let His Spirit strengthen your spirit.

Make your own breaks.

It's a funny thing. The more I practice, the luckier I get.

—Arnold Palmer

PREPARATION

Many years ago, a member of the Japanese emperor commissioned a painting of a bird. After many months had passed, the artist still had not produced the painting. The emperor became impatient and called for the artist. Rather than explain why he had not already created the painting, the artist simply went to a blank canvass and set to work. Within an hour he had completed an exquisite masterpiece. When pressed to explain the delay, the artist displayed numerous drawings of talons, beaks, and feathers. Only because he had done such extensive preparation could the artist complete the painting so quickly.

There is no such thing as an overnight success or instant results. The athletes whose performance seems the most effortless are those who have spent the longest time in training. Practice, practice, practice. This is the secret to outstanding performance. The same is true in every area of your life. Mentally, spiritually, and relationally, those who grow are those who invest the time in discipline, learning, and applying truth to life.

Do you want to become an overnight sensation? You can, if you are willing to first invest thousands of days and nights in preparing yourself for victory. It takes many hours of work to enjoy a few

Find out what works.

A heavy hitter is nothing more than a little hitter who kept on hitting.

—Pete Zafra

PERSISTENCE

Have you ever seen a stonecutter at work? These craftsmen shape stones that are useable in building from the massive raw rocks that come from a quarry. A skilled cutter may hammer at a rock one hundred times without so much as a single crack showing in it. Yet at the one-hundred-first blow, the stone will split in two, exactly along the fault line that the cutter had in mind. It is not the single blow that splits the stone but the weight of all the accumulated effort. It takes a great deal of persistence to shape a stone.

In your athletic career, you will face periods where the seems to be little gain for your effort. You results will taper off. Your workouts will seem to plateau. It will seem as if there is no point in gearing up for one more effort. Remember the lesson of the stonecutter. It isn't the single stroke that gets results; it is the weight of all your accumulated effort that will finally pay off.

Find a rhythm that works, then stick with it. Do not expect to drop your times by a dramatic margin. Be content with small but steady gains. Don't become discouraged if you do not achieve immediate results. Remember that it takes time to move mountains, split rocks, or fine tune the human body. Keep working. Your effort will bring results in the end.

Consider the impact of your choices.

Go to the ant, you sluggard.

Consider its ways and be wise!

—Proverbs 6:6

WISDOM

One day an angel appeared to a coach in the clubhouse and told him that in return for his exemplary behavior, the Lord was going to reward him with his choice of infinite wealth, perfect wisdom, or matchless beauty. Without hesitation, the coach chose infinite wisdom.

"Done!" the angel said, and disappeared in a cloud of smoke and bolt of lightning. After a moment, all the players turned toward the coach, who now sat surrounded by a halo of light. After awhile, the team captain tapped him on the shoulder and said, "Coach, say something."

The coach looked at them and said, "I should have taken the money."

Every day you make dozens of choices that have an impact upon your future. You must choose when to get up, what to eat, when to train, how long to work, what to say, which opportunities to pursue and which to ignore, which e-mails to answer and which to delete, and many more. All of your choices add up to a single, much larger, choice—how you will live your life.

Consider carefully the impact of each choice you make. Choose discipline over selfishness. Choose kindness over convenience. Choose character over compromise. Wisdom is seeing the long-term impact of the choices you make. Choose to live the life you want tomorrow—not simply what feels good today.

Focus on the goal.

Don't look back. Something might
be gaining on you.

—Satchel Paige

FUTURE

Yesterday is a closed box. It is a museum piece encased in glass. You can take it out and look at it, but you can never open the lid. You cannot change the past. The day in which you can take action is today. The day that you can change is tomorrow. If you are to succeed in any endeavor you must be future focused.

Too often we waste precious time and mental energy fretting over the things we cannot change. We lament the training we did not do rather than heading to the gym. We punish ourselves for the play we failed to make or the shot we didn't take rather than training for the next event. While it is important to be instructed by our mistakes, it is an even greater mistake to be consumed by them. In sports and in life, it is important to put the past behind us and focus on the future.

Stop worrying about your performance in the last contest, prepare for the next one. Don't allow the things you did, failed to do, or should have done prevent you from doing the things that you *can* do right now. Your best days are not behind you; they are yet to come.

Get in the zone.

Concentration is a fine

antidote to anxiety.

—Jack Nicklaus

CONCENTRATION

Every athlete needs this. There is no sport that does not require it. The golfer standing on the eighteenth green, surrounded by a gallery of fans, needs this quality in order to sink a putt. The offensive lineman needs it, lined up for the third-down snap in a stadium reverberating with the sound of eighty-thousand cheering fans. The marathoner needs it in order to keep her eyes on the finish line, still eight miles away. It is concentration, the ability to shut out all distractions and focus on the one thing that matters most.

Every day you have many priorities competing for your attention. Your career demands a lot of time, your family needs your energy, your friends need some attention, your sport requires your investment. It is impossible to juggle these priorities. You cannot keep them all in your sights at the same time. You must choose which area to focus on at any given moment—then give it your full attention. You are not being unfaithful to your other priorities by setting them aside for a brief time.

When you are at the dinner table, forget about your next workout and focus on your family. When you are at the computer, ignore the Facebook updates from your friends and crank out the work. And when you are in the gym, on the road, or in the pool, *concentrate*! Force distractions from your mind, and get into the zone. You must focus in order to achieve.

Train hard.

Genius is one percent inspiration and ninety-nine percent perspiration.

—Thomas Edison

SWEAT

Sweating is actually good for you. Not only does the act of sweating cool you, thereby regulating your body's temperature, but it also helps to cleanse your body by removing waste and toxins. Working up a good sweat is one of the healthiest things you can do!

Too often we buy the notion that good results can be achieved with little effort. There are many hucksters out there selling get-thin-quick diets or ten easy steps to success. It is tempting to think that we can get to the top of our sport by practicing only when we feel like it, lifting only what's within our range, and never pushing beyond our previous best. Everyone wants to cross the finish line, but not everyone wants to sweat.

If you are going to succeed as an athlete, or in life, you will need to forget the notion that achievement will come with little effort. There is no shortcut to the finish line. You will need to work hard in order to achieve. That is true in the gym and on the court. It is also true in your profession, in your family, and in your spiritual life. Growth in any area requires disciplined effort. So go ahead, work up a sweat. It'll be good for you.

Finish.

A lot of people run a race to see who is fastest. I run to see who has the most guts, who can punish himself into exhausting pace, and then at the end, punish himself even more.

—Steve Prefontaine

PERSEVERANCE

The Tour de France is the most prestigious bicycle race in the world. Each July it winds its way through the hillsides, vineyards, and mountain peaks of France covering more than two thousand miles in twenty-one days of racing. To win the Tour is the achievement of a lifetime. Yet because the race is so demanding, merely to finish the three-week event is an achievement in itself. In recognition of the grueling nature of this contest, the organizers annually award another award besides the coveted winner's yellow jersey. The *lantern rouge,* or red lantern, is awarded to the *last* man to finish the tour. This award signifies that the ride has worked hard, probably sacrificing his own chances at victory for the sake of a teammate. Though the race was punishing, he hung on.

The apostle Paul paints a similar picture of his own life, saying, "One thing I do: Forgetting what is behind and straining toward what is ahead, I press on toward the goal to win the prize for which God has called me heavenward in Christ Jesus (Philippians 3:14–15). Your life is a marathon, not a sprint. To finish well, you will need perseverance more than raw passion, staying power more than speed. When the going gets tough, keep going. Remain faithful, stay strong.

About the Authors

Dr. Stan A. Toler is general superintendent in the Church of the Nazarene with an office at the Global Ministry Center in Lenexa, Kansas.

Stan Toler has written over 80 books, including his best-sellers, *God Has Never Failed Me, But He's Sure Scared Me to Death a Few Times*; *The Buzzards Are Circling, But God's Not Finished With Me Yet*; *God's Never Late, He's Seldom Early, He's Always Right on Time*; *The Secret Blend*; *Richest Person in the World*; *Practical Guide to Pastoral Ministry*; *The Inspirational Speaker's Resource, ReThink Your Life,* his popular Minute Motivator series, *If Only I Could Relate To The People I'm Related To* and his newest book, *God Can Do Anything But Fail: So Try Parasailing In A Windstorm.*

Toler recently was honored with a honorary Doctorate of Divinity from Southern Nazarene University.

He and his wife, Linda, an educator, have two married sons, Seth (Marcy) and Adam (Amanda), and two grandsons Rhett and Davis.

www.stantoler.com

Billy Bajema is currently a tight end for the St. Louis Rams. He was originally drafted by the San Francisco 49ers in the 7th round of the NFL draft. He has played in 97 NFL games with 42 career starts. While attending Oklahoma State University he received the first ever National Bobby Bowden Award given by the Fellowship of Christian Athletes to one college football player for their achievement on the field and in the classroom and for their conduct as a faith model in the community. Billy and his wife Emily have three children, Will, Ben, and Audrey-Kate.